PRANK star

100 JOKES AND PRANKS

by Tim Bugbird

This book is all you need to fill your days with joking joy!

Record and rate your pranks in the section at the back and remember: practice makes a

Prank Star!

Absolutely not for anyone who's old enough to know better!

RULES OF PRANKING

1 Never play a prank on a complete stranger – you never know how they might react!

2 Pick your victims with care and consideration – pranking your 90-year-old neighbor is **not** funny. (Pranking your best friend *is* funny.)

3 Most pranks require practice. Make sure you've perfected the prank before you spring the surprise!

4 If you play practical jokes, you have to be prepared to be pranked back. Make sure you can see the funny side!

5 Spread the fun! If you keep pranking the same person, your pranks will cease to be surprising!

6 Check to make sure that your victims have no allergies before carrying out pranks involving food.

7 If your prank is messy, clean up when it's over.

1

WHOSE CAT DID THAT?

Fake puke is easy to make and great for livening up boring family parties or visits to the grocery store.

You will need:
PVA glue
plastic wrap
an old magazine
a cookie or cracker

First crush the cookie. Be sure to have a good mix of chunky bits and fine, crumbly pieces.

Place the plastic wrap flat on the magazine. Squirt a blob of glue onto the plastic wrap, then sprinkle the crushed cookie on top.

Leave for at least a day then gently peel the fake puke from the wrap.

2

What did the sausage say to the bacon?

I HAM so pleased to MEAT you!

3

EEEEK!

Where does a skunk do its washing up?

In the kitchen **STINK!**

TOILET TROUBLE PART 1

4

Make nature's call a moment to remember with this perfect prank!

When no one is looking, sneak into the bathroom and remove the roll of toilet paper.

Using a hole punch, make a generous handful of paper dots. Roll out about six sheets of toilet paper and scatter dots on the paper until you are two sheets from the end.

Next, carefully roll the paper back up and hook it on the toilet-roll holder. When your victim pulls at the roll, they'll find themselves showered in tiny dots!

Go to number 20 for more fun with paper dots and number 57 for extra toilet-paper pranking!

5

What did the kettle say when the pan lost his temper?

Just SIMMER down!

BIG FOOT!

This prank is perfect for hot summer days.

Begin the prank by telling your victim you've read about how, in the summer, the heat makes people's feet grow bigger. Ask them if they've ever heard this, then change the subject. The next day, take a rolled-up handkerchief or sock and stuff it in the toes of your victim's shoes. Let the laughs roll in as they think their feet have ballooned!

6

Spaghetti Trees!

One of the most famous April Fool's pranks of all time was on British TV over 50 years ago. The news show Panorama showed farmers in Switzerland picking strings of spaghetti from their "spaghetti trees." Viewers all over the country phoned in to ask where they could buy the trees so they could grow their own!

DUH!

8

5 excellent uses for a
whoopee cushion

1 Slip it under the cushion of your dad's chair.

2 Give it a squeeze just as everyone sits down for a nice family lunch.

3 How about ripping a parp at the dentist's?

4 Or leaving it under a cushion in your sister's bedroom?

5 Punk your pal by leaving a cushion on his seat at the movies – it's so dark, he'll never see it coming!

SECRET CODES

If you want to be **King of Pranks**, you need to keep your secrets safe, and the best way is to create your own code.

Try using this back-to-front alphabet. Instead of A, you write Z, instead of B, you write Y, and so on.

A	B	C	D	E	F	G	H	I	J	K	L	M
Z	Y	X	W	V	U	T	S	R	Q	P	O	N

N	O	P	Q	R	S	T	U	V	W	X	Y	Z
M	L	K	J	I	H	G	F	E	D	C	B	A

Instead of letters, you could use shapes, numbers, or a mix of all three.

Try creating your own secret prank codes.

10

What did the dice say when the cards refused to shuffle?

I'LL DEAL WITH YOU LATER!

11

Doctor, Doctor!
I think I'm a yo-yo!

How do you feel?

Sometimes I'm up and
sometimes I'm down!

12

FREAKY FINGER

ARGH!

Tell your victim you've found something interesting on the sidewalk and ask him or her to open the box. LOL as your victim shrieks at the sight of your festering finger!

Find some cotton balls (enough to fill most of the box), dab them with dark red paint, and let them dry.

Find a small gift box and cut a hole in the bottom large enough to stick your finger through.

Cup the box in your hand, placing your middle finger through the hole, and pad the box with the cotton balls. Put the lid on the box.

Offer the box to your friends and wiggle your finger as they lift the lid!

OOPS!

13 Where do smelly dinosaurs live?

JURASSIC PARP!

14

THE DO NOTHING PRANK

Here's a way to punk your pals by doing absolutely NOTHING.

A couple of days before April 1st, tell your pal you've heard of some really amazing April Fool's Day pranks. A little later, say you've thought up the most awesome prank ever, but refuse to share it. The next day, say you're just trying to decide who to pull the prank on. When it comes to April 1st, do nothing, but every time you see your pal smirk, look the other way or do something to look suspicious – for example, keep looking at his bag in a way that suggests you put something in it or you are about to! All the while, do nothing – the prank is that your pal spent the day thinking he was about to be pranked!

15

Do you want fries with that?

In 1998, Burger King® pranked all of America when it advertised a new Whopper® with its contents rearranged especially for the country's left-handed folk. Thousands of customers asked for a left-handed lunch, only to be told it was a complete hoax!

DUH!

16

Which noses are super fit?

Ones that are always **running!**

MOVE-IT-AROUND MAYHEM!

This top gag is perfect to play on your sister or brother!

Sneak into your brother or sister's room and simply move things around a little. For example, switch the books on the bookshelf so they are in a different order, rearrange the contents of their drawers, or move their ornaments or trophies onto a different shelf. They may not notice the changes at first, but if they do, deny all knowledge and make a note to make some more changes the following day!

After two days, reveal your prank or the confusion may make them completely crazy!

18

What goes
HA! HA! BONK!

A man laughing
his head off!

OOPS!

19 Why did the toilet turn red?

Because it felt a little FLUSHED!

SNOW JOKE

20 This is a classic prank – perfect for a rainy day!

Find a hole punch and punch as many holes as you can before you get completely bored or your wrist aches.

Find an umbrella and open it slightly.

Pour the punched holes carefully into the umbrella and roll it back up, tightly.

Wait for your victim to open up the umbrella, and then roll on the floor laughing when he or she is showered with tiny paper dots!

SHOWER YOUR FRIENDS WITH JOY!

Why was the pony whispering?

Because he was a little HORSE!

SPRINGY SURPRISE!

22

Make opening a book a springy surprise!

Find a thick, OLD book – that is, one that no one wants. If it's not yours, ASK first! A hardback book is best for this prank.

Draw a circle about 1 1/4 in (3 cm) in diameter in the middle of the first page and use this as a guide to cut a hole about 80 pages deep. Cut several pages at a time and use the hole you have cut to draw more cutting guides. Next, cut a strip of cardboard about 5 7/8 in (15 cm) long and 3/8 in (1 cm) wide. Fold the cardboard back and forth every 3/8 in (1 cm) to form a spring. Now cut a circle of cardboard just bigger than the hole. Draw something gross like a bug or an eyeball on the circle and stick it on the spring.

Fold the spring up, place it in the hole, and carefully close the book. Hand the book to a friend, explaining that there is something completely fascinating on the first page. Point the book in your friend's direction so he or she looks, and then open the cover quickly to give your friend a springy surprise!

ARGH!

POINNNG!

123

real life prank fact . . . real life prank fact . . .

Coffee Caper

In 2010, Starbucks® coffee shops pranked their customers by announcing two new cup sizes – an extra-small, 2-oz (50-ml) cup for customers who just wanted a sip, and a super-sized, 128-oz (3.5-l) cup for extra-thirsty coffee lovers. The new big cups would be so big that customers could reuse them as lampshades or hats, while the sipping cups would make perfect egg cups or paperclip holders!

124

WHAT DID THE BED SAY WHEN THE CURTAINS STARTED CRYING?

JUST PULL YOURSELF TOGETHER!

25

This classic gag fools 'em every time!

1) Bend the tops of both thumbs inward as far as you can.

2) Place your thumbs together so that the bottom half of one thumb joins with the top half of the other.

3) Wrap a forefinger around the "join" between your two thumbs.

4) Raise the top half of your new thumb slowly and stifle your smirks as your friends are fooled into believing that your thumb has broken in two!

TOP TIP! Practice different hand-finger combinations to perfect your prank!

OUCH!

26

Why did the fork fall out with the spoon?

Because it kept STIRRING things up!

27

How do you stop your phone battery from running out?

Hide its **sneakers**!

HILARIOUS HANKIES!

28

A great prank to play on your brother or sister, but you'll need an adult to help.

Simply sew the corner of a handkerchief into the bottom of your subject's coat or in a pocket of his or her pants.

Then laugh your pants off when your sib fails to pull the pesky rag from his or her pocket!

THAT'S *NOT* FUNNY!

29

Which vampire lives in a kitchen drawer?

Count SPATULA!

30

STICKY SAUCE!

Roll on the floor laughing when your family's feast is stalled by unsqueezable sauce!

Just before dinner, collect all the squeeze sauce and mayo bottles. Unscrew the tops and use them as templates to make card discs to fit neatly inside the lids. Screw the lids back on, put the sauces on the table, and sit back and enjoy the show – no amount of squeezing will release the tasty toppings!

TOP TIP! For an extra-special effect, color the card to match the sauce!

31

Hothead!

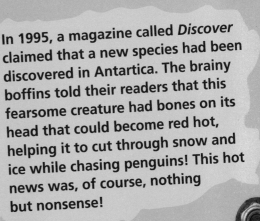

In 1995, a magazine called *Discover* claimed that a new species had been discovered in Antartica. The brainy boffins told their readers that this fearsome creature had bones on its head that could become red hot, helping it to cut through snow and ice while chasing penguins! This hot news was, of course, nothing but nonsense!

32

Waiter, Waiter!

There's a twig in my soup!

Then talk to our BRANCH manager!

HUH?!

33

A surefire way to keep 'em clueless!

Fox your folks and keep your shenanigans secret by giving words alternative meanings. For example, instead of saying "boring," you could say "raspberry": "Oh my, math is SO raspberry today!"

Make up your own PRANK STAR language here!

Word	Prank Language

34

What do you get if you put your pen in the freezer?
Iced ink?
Well yes, you do, but that wasn't the question!

35

Where did the worm leave its dog?

Tied to the caterPILLAR!

36 MAGGOT ATTACK!

It's so simple to fool your folks into believing that their lovely fruit bowl has been invaded by insects!

Simply take an apple from the fruit bowl and, using a sharp pencil, make holes all around it. Leave the apple for a few hours and the holes will become nice and brown. Then return the fruit and scatter a few fake bugs around the bowl. Watch your mom howl in horror when she reaches for her favorite fruit!

37

Why was the skeleton feeling lonely?

Sniff!

Because he had NO BODY to play with!

38

WHAT BARKING NONSENSE!

Animal Antics!

In 2010, Google took online pranking to a new level when it announced the "Translate for Animals" app. A special webpage announced that soon we'd be able to understand what our pets were saying with translators for dogs, chickens, sheep, and even tortoises!

THAT'S TORN IT!

39

This prank is almost too easy to be true and scores a straight A for maximum laughs at minimum effort!

Find an old piece of cloth and make small cuts around the edges – this will make the cloth easy to rip. Wait for a friend to bend over, then swiftly rip the rag, and delight in your pal thinking they've torn their pants!

40

Why was the hen banned from the Internet chatroom?

!!*!

Because her language was so fowl!

(41)

Have your family in a spin by turning the clocks forward.

This prank is best performed on a day when everyone's home so the joke can be enjoyed by all! Get up early (difficult but worth the trouble) and move as many clocks as you can forward by three hours. Stand back and watch the scramble when everyone thinks they are late for their important appointments!

ZOOOM

(42)

Why was the meatball tired?

Because it was **pasta** its bedtime!

YAWN!

43

Why did the fool cut a hole in his umbrella?

So he could see when it stopped raining!

44

DON'T DO THAT!

The best way to prank a pal into punking themselves is to tell them ABSOLUTELY not to do something!

If you say "don't," chances are the temptation will be just too much! The secret is to advise strongly against doing something really simple (like opening a book or cupboard) and then surprise your pal with a crazy consequence when the temptation becomes just too strong! Always leave your instruction on a large sticky note where it can't be missed! For example:

"Do NOT open page 52!" (Cover page 52 in hole-punch dots, and then carefully close the book.)

"This cupboard door must be kept CLOSED at all times!" (Hang plastic bugs and other freaky finds on the inside of the door frame.)

"Do not remove this newspaper!" (Sneak a splat of homemade puke under the paper for a sickening surprise!)

Where's the best place to make a noise online?

CRASH

The DIN-ternet

MOVING MONEY!

Prank your pals as they make for the money!

Attach a coin to a long piece of black cotton and place it on a table. Sit at the table with something light, like a piece of paper, covering the cotton trail, and keep your hand underneath the table holding the end of the thread. Wait for your pal to join you at the table, and then the moment he makes a dash for the cash, pull the cotton. Watch him jump out of his skin as the money escapes his greedy grasp!

BIG YAWN!

47

Send your pals to sleep with one of the simplest pranks ever!

The next time you're with a group of friends or at a family party, see if you can set off a train of tirdness by simply yawning! Yawn just a little at first, then after a minute or two, yawn a little louder and longer. Watch to see if anyone else yawns, and then yawn some more! Before long, the rest of the room will be sent into a snooze!

YAWN!!!!!!!!

48

What did the frog order from the burger bar?

A CROAK and FLIES!

ROTTEN RATHERS!

Would you rather . . .

Have triple math homework . . . **or** . . . kiss your best friend's sister?

eat your own nail clippings . . . **or** . . . put your hands in a bag of raw fish?

put a ferret down your pants . . . **or** . . . lick the bottom of your shoe?

wear your underwear on the outside . . . **or** . . . clean your sister's bedroom?

change your name to Doreen . . . **or** . . . grow an extra ear?

What's a cow's favorite kind of show?

A **MOO**-sical

51

What did the queen bee say when the worker bees started messing around?

Oh, do BEE-HIVE!

52

real life prank fact . . . real life prank fact . . .

Crazy color

Years ago in Sweden, when all TV shows were shown in black and white, an expert announced that viewers could convert their TVs to color by simply pulling an old nylon stocking over the screen! Seems some silly Swedes thought it was a great idea and were surprised when the stocking netted no results!

53

Why didn't the snowman go to the disco?

Because he had tickets to the snow ball!

54

FAKE BOOGER!

Another cunning use of PVA glue – sure to delight friends and relatives alike!

You will need: PVA glue · an old magazine · an old pencil · green paint · plastic wrap

Place the plastic wrap on the magazine.

Squirt a blob of glue on the plastic wrap.

Mix up a little green paint (or yellow, or both) and put a few drops on the glue blob.

Use your pencil to mix the paint gently into the glue and create a nice booger shape.

Leave it to dry for at least a day.

Gently peel the booger off the plastic wrap.

(Now go to number 92)

55

WHAT A PAIN!

CRAAAAAAAACK

Ever been told not to kick a ball in the house in case you BREAK A WINDOW? Prank your parents into believing you've done just that!

Take a piece of plastic wrap and smooth it over a table or countertop. Using a black permanent marker, draw zigzag lines over the wrap. Now gently apply the plastic to a handy window, grab your ball, and fess up!

TOP TIP

A window with lace curtains or a slatted blind will work best because they help hide creases in the plastic wrap!

56

Why did the monster eat the flashlight?

He wanted a **light snack!**

57 TOILET TROUBLE PART 2

There's nothing like being punk'd when you're minding your own business!

When no one is looking, take the roll of toilet paper from the bathroom. Replace it with a new roll until you are ready (so no one gets suspicious).

Unroll three sheets and put a few dots of glue on the third sheet. Roll it back up, press the glued area lightly, and leave it to dry.

Once the glue is totally dry, roll the paper back up and put it in the holder with the first two sheets left dangling. Wait for your victim to answer nature's call, and then listen to him or her wail when the roll won't unravel!

PARP!

58

Why did the brainiac eat her homework? Because it was a piece of cake!

TEE HEE!

How do you make milkshake? Say, **"BOO!"**

BOO!

Highflier!

Not all pranks go according to plan. In 1989, famous businessman Richard Branson had a hot-air balloon made to look like a flying saucer. The plan was to land in London's Hyde Park on April Fool's Day. Many motorists were fooled by the curious craft floating toward the city, but the prank fell flat when a change in the weather forced Branson to land a day early in a field outside London!

61

What color are hiccups?

BURPLE!

62

SEW SNEAKY!

If you got endless joy from the Hilarious Handkerchief (prank 28), go one step further and spring a morning surprise on your favorite brother or sister!

IMPORTANT! This prank definitely requires some grown-up help and permission!

While your victim is out of the house, raid his or her drawers for a nice selection of socks and underwear. With a needle and thread, gently join them together with one or two stitches to create a chain of clothes, and then neatly place them back in the drawer.

The next morning, keep a joyful ear to the bedroom door as your bleary-eyed sibling reaches out and grabs a string of socks or a parade of underpants!

63

WHAT'S THAT?!

A super-easy prank to get your friends staring.

All you do is stand still, then look up and point.
Wait for a few seconds, then lower your hand, walk
on, and then look over your shoulder at the fools
staring at the sky, wondering what you saw!

Great places to perform this prank include:

the park
a playground
the shopping mall
on a busy sidewalk
the zoo

GASP!

TOP TIP! Combine your pointing with a look
of horror, joy, or confusion to really get 'em looking!

64

What did the sun say to the
cloud when he went on vacation?
You'll be MIST!

CEREAL SWITCH!

65

What could be merrier than causing mealtime mayhem at the breakfast table?

The night before you spring your surprise, sneak into the kitchen and swap the inside bags of everyone's favorite cereals.

Perfect your plan by sealing any squeeze bottles (see prank 30) and giving them a milky surprise (see prank 89)!

The next morning, step back, act dumb, and let the chaos commence!

66

WHY WAS THE HORSE SMELLY?

BECAUSE THE COW GAVE HIM A PAT ON THE BACK!

67

What did the man say when he put on a coat made of sausages?

Dinner's on me!

68

The Australian Iceberg

Everyone was excited when Australian businessman Dick Smith announced that he was going to tow an iceberg into Sydney Harbor. The massive ice mountain was to be broken up into small cubes to sell at 10 cents each, and crowds gathered to see it being towed in. But a rain shower put an end to the prank, revealing the "iceberg" to be nothing but a pile of foam on top of some white sheets!

69

How do fishermen catch virtual fish?

Online!

70

Whistle while you work!

On April 1st, 2002, the British supermarket Tesco printed a newspaper ad for a specially produced whistling carrot. This crafty carrot had holes in the side, which would make the veg blow like a whistle when beautifully boiled! **DUH!**

HONK!

FUNNY FILLINGS!

HEE-HEE!

Thrill your friends with some dreadful donuts!

Take two donuts and carefully make a hole in the bottom of one using the end of a teaspoon handle. Next, squirt a little mayo or tomato sauce on the end of the spoon handle and push it into the donut. Finally, put both donuts on a plate and offer one to a friend, being careful to take your 'nut first. Enjoy your sweet treat as your friend munches in misery!

72

What do elves do after school?

Their gnomework!

73

BEDTIME BEASTLINESS!

Give someone special a bedtime bonus!

Just before bedtime, sneak into your brother's or sister's room and pile some surprises under the sheets. Old shoes, for example, would make a fabulous find, as would a few crunchy cornflakes (be prepared to have to clean them up) or an old frying pan. Make the prank extra memorable by hiding the goodies UNDER the bottom sheet! Sweet dreams!

EEEEK!

74

Why was the shirt sad?

Because the jeans were BLUE!

75

Have you seen the new onion website?

Yes, it's a SITE for sore eyes!

76

ROTTEN RATHERS!

Would you rather . . .

Pour a bucket of slugs over your head . . . **or** . . . eat a snail sandwich?

Sit in a bathtub full of snakes . . . **or** . . . dye your hair green?

Run around school in your underwear . . . **or** . . . have 6 math detentions?

Fill your pockets with cockroaches . . . **or** . . . fill your shoes with maggots?

Lie on a bed of nails . . . **or** . . . lie on a bed of worms?

Drink a pint of bathwater . . . **or** . . . drink a pint of pond water?

77

Doctor, Doctor,
I caught a cold!

Achoo!

Then throw it
back, you fool!

78

Can Penguins Fly?

Of course they can't! But that didn't stop the BBC from airing a nature show in 2008 showing just that! The program explained that, rather than put up with Antarctic winters, the perky penguins flew to the South American rain forests to enjoy the sun. Viewers were amazed to see the waddling wonders soaring through the sky – then later they were shown how it was done with special effects and camera trickery!

79

TOP 5 USES FOR PLASTIC CRITTERS

1 Scatter freely in your sister's underwear drawer.

2 Hide one under the TV remote.

3 Tie to pieces of black cotton and dangle them from door frames.

4 Hide them in your friends' shoes.

5 Drop one on your sister's head when she's not looking and see how long it takes her to find it tangled in her lovely locks!

80

HMMM?

Why did the woman put blush on her forehead?

She was trying to make up her mind!

DISGUSTING DIGIT!

81

Creep out your little brother with your "spare" finger!

Take a small foam or cardboard cup with a lid and make a hole in the bottom big enough to stick your finger through. Put the middle finger of either hand through the hole and practice folding your fingers so it looks as though you are holding the cup in the palm of your hand. Put the lid on the cup and carry a book or bag in your other hand. Ask your brother to open the cup for you (because your hands are full) and as he opens the cup, wiggle your finger to give him the fright of his life!

82

"TO BE OR NOT TO BE"

Why did the bottom become an actor?
It wanted a leading PARP!

83

Why doesn't Tarzan need a calculator?

Because the jungle is full of **ADDERS**!

5+2+7

34 SLIPPERY PENCILS!

Take a little liquid soap and smear it lightly over the barrels of two or three pencils. Place the pencils on a work surface and challenge a friend to a game of hangman. Offer your friend a pencil, and then join in the fun as he or she fails to get a grip!

85

Why are hairdressers always cheating?

Because they make shortcuts!

86

COOKIES 'N' SCREAM!

If filling a donut with a freaky flavor was just too much fun, try this cookie-based caper for a load more laughs!

Take a selection of sandwich-style cookies and gently open them up. Add an edible (but unexpected) flavor to the cream filling – for example, a sprinkling of salt and pepper or a little mayo – then carefully put the cookies back together. Offer your friends a tasty treat, then watch their faces fall as they sample the terrible taste!

87

Moving monument

In 1986, a French newspaper made the shocking – and totally untrue – announcement that the famous Eiffel Tower would be taken down and moved to become an attraction at the new Disney park in Paris!

OOH LA LA!

88

Why did the man take a clock on the plane?

He wanted to see time fly!

MILKY WAY!

89

This is a classic breakfast-time prank that always creates a stir! Simply add a few drops of green food coloring to a carton of milk, shake the carton gently, then place it on the table and let your family enjoy the sour-looking surprise!

YUK!

90

How do you make a hat stand?

Take away its chair!

91

Why did the broom get married so fast?

Because she was swept off her feet!

92

5 excellent things to do with a **fake booger**

(see prank 54)

(Note! Before pranking, make sure the paint will not rub off on anything!)

1 Leave it on top of your mom's lovely clean laundry.

2 Place it gently next to your sister's fork at the dinner table.

3 See if you can make it hang from your nose, and then go to school without it falling off.

4 Place it on the palm of your hand, then shake hands with a pal or random relative.

5 Stick one on the side of a packet of cookies, then offer them to a favorite aunt.

93

Why did the nose hate team sports?

Because he never got picked!

94

Metric madness

In 1975, an Australian news show announced that the country would be moving to "metric time." This meant that instead of 60 seconds, there would be 100 seconds in a minute and 100 minutes in an hour. To make matters even crazier, there would be 20 hours in a day, seconds would be renamed "millidays," and hours, "decidays." They even showed a new clock with 10 hours on its face!

95 ALARMING!

There's nothing worse than being woken up when you are having a nice snooze, so why not give a "loved one" (that is, your older sister or younger brother) this treat by hiding an alarm clock in his or her room? Set the clock nice and early and hide it somewhere they wouldn't think to look. Be sure the clock hasn't got a loud tick, or you may be rumbled!

IT'S ALL ABOUT TIMING!

96

Why was the whisk sent to jail?

For beating the eggs!

OUCH

97

Leave a sticky Prank Star note by the phone and see who picks up the message!

Things look a bit fishy – please call Ann Chovie

The house is a mess – please call Dustin D. Furnicha

Found a great place for our vacation – please call Candice B. dePlace

We're out of food – please call Hammond Egz

98

What kind of vegetables do you find in the gym?

Muscle sprouts!

99

Why did the tomato blush?

Because he saw the salad dressing!

100

real life prank fact . . . real life prank fact . . .

What's lurking in the loch?

For years, people have believed that a sea monster lives in the waters of Loch Ness in Scotland. In 1972, many thought evidence had finally been found when a 15.5-ft (4.7-m) carcass was seen floating in the chilly loch. This deep-water discovery made the news all over the world, but it soon turned out to be an enormous bull elephant seal, which had been placed in the waters as an April Fool's joke!

PRANK LOG

Prank number	WHO did you prank?	Date	Score (out of 10)

PRANK LOG

Prank number	WHO did you prank?	Date	Score (out of 10)

PRANK LOG

Prank number	WHO did you prank?	Date	Score (out of 10)

PRANK LOG

Prank number	WHO did you prank?	Date	Score (out of 10)

PRANK LOG

Prank number	WHO did you prank?	Date	Score (out of 10)

PRANK LOG

Prank number	WHO did you prank?	Date	Score (out of 10)